C000246683

Nicki Jackowska has published six collections of poetry, three novels and the groundbreaking book on language, *Write for Life*. She works as a creative writing tutor and advisor, collaborates with visual artists, and is a consummate performer of her poetry, drawing upon early theatrical roots. Her intimate knowledge of theatre is reflected in *Behold* and in her recently completed novel, *The Lost Gardens of Mariamne*. Jackowska has received a Lannan Grant and an Arts Council England grant. She lives and works in Brighton.

Nicki Jackowska

BEHOLD

ENITHARMON PRESS

First published in 2009
by Enitharmon Press
26B Caversham Road
London NW5 2DU

www.enitharmon.co.uk

Distributed in the UK by
Central Books
99 Wallis Road
London E9 5LN

Distributed in the USA and Canada
by Dufour Editions Inc.
PO Box 7, Chester Springs
PA 19425, USA

ISBN: 978-1-904634-85-0

Enitharmon Press gratefully acknowledges the financial support of
Arts Council England, London.

British Library Cataloguing-in-Publication Data.
A catalogue record for this book is available
from the British Library.

Designed in Albertina by Libanus Press
and printed in England by
Antony Rowe Ltd

*for Seamus and Morgan
and their great-great-grandmother
Elsie Lilian Lucas*

ACKNOWLEDGEMENTS

Some of these poems have appeared in the following magazines: *Foolscap, Leviathan Quarterly, London Magazine, PN Review, Poetry London, Stand.*

'Magpie' was written during a residency at the Indigo exhibition, Brighton Museum and Art Gallery.

'Between Us' was published by Pratt Contemporary Art 2005 as a limited edition.

CONTENTS

BETWEEN US

for Paula Rego, *Jane Eyre and Other Stories*
Marlborough Fine Art, October 2003

1   Paula, this letter is not meant in homage
    nor to repeat that gesture made last night
    when playfully I pressed my head deep
    in the hollow of your shoulder, monkey-wise
    to say I'm no homunculus but just for
    one evening, prepared to be your sprite.

2   This evening when a heavy glass door opens,
    lets the rabble in for concourse with your art,
    a new collection, Jane Eyre as never seen, a Rochester
    undone and sulky, glowering for his reconciliation,
    Bertha the very weight of madness turned up high –
    a loved and classic tale breaks its locks and moans.

3   I recognise that monkey, that thick red curtain
    the hand stroking thread and hair, drawing
    the night off from the day; my stories break
    cover, leap out and cleave the canvas, you
    have echoed my impertinence, insects and all,
    you have conjured Bertha's monkey on my attic wall.

4   This cloth you bear, this curtain, rust and ore,
    Jane is the woman who can dare it, draw
    it back. My Mariamne stalks your corridor
    in hot pursuit, her body riddled with
    the specimens she maps and names by day.
    So does imagination pierce the flesh, the clay.

5   Between the rolling, darkening hills of Wales
    and these bright rhymes, your child's unstoppable
    unfolding – a rope is coiled together in the space
    between my hinterland and your thick pastels.
    A contradiction, they are dark as blood, not faded out
    as pastel would suggest but livid as an icon is.

6   For all our heroines are grappling unseen against
    a flood too great for stoppage; only the edge
    of paper, frame or wall can keep them in.
    Mine light a fuse upon the air and rush to greet
    the sisters, sprawled and taunting, pacing these walls.
    The air is thick, unwritten chapters flap their wings.

7   Between your painting and my eye, a river runs
    fish-full and turbulent; each contributes line,
    hook, bait; standing in solemn contemplation
    of each other, your painted thighs sink deep
    and I'm astride the silk-road, swimming hard
    upstream, lying with a monkey in the crease.

8   This is one encounter, *coniuctio* in passing
    for all this show will poke and pry among
    the stones that labour at the bottom of the sea
    to hold their secrets; few stick it out,
    the current's strong. I blend my tide with yours,
    from underneath a gross menagerie blinks and creeps

9   in watery light, the blind forgotten army we
    were cursed with when our childhood innocence
    took flight and no words came to cup and rescue us,
    no good godmothers to take the splinter out
    and furless bunny-rabbits tempt the edge of human
    in their sport; you call it war, true face of the child.

10   Paula, I have an army of my own,
        a choir, an insect house, a sawdust ring,
        place of a thousand cages hosting heaven's cast-offs,
        dressing rooms of play that go too far
        and can't be stopped and end in tears –
        or should I say the shifting shapes of terror.

11   Beak in her mouth I taste, my own teeth lodged
        in a rabbit's snarl. Your images set foot
        upon us, bring us to heel. Rochester's shiny boot
        taps a toe in warning; forces us to feel each itch
        and rupture, join of flesh and mask. I search that precious
        border; these are pictures on a wall, without me barren.

INTO THE TOMB

You'd have thought we were moving
in the opposite direction, stonewards
kicking out love and bridges,
the very name we'd forged to live by.
It's all the same to you if
this or that shape of me lies
aloft or begotten; we'd forgotten
Christmas, the tender need, raw
chances down the phone, a pitch and
toss too fine to catch, fugitive
those sound-waves lining your
base voice I am bewitched by.
Never lie too close will you
undoing time like an easy zip-up
dress I slip from, and go from
you naked as a lover might
except I move in the opposite
direction, which is where we started
breaking the usual mould; and when I
move as though called to your door
meaning to leave with something more
than hate, come you say and the vivid
place of you folds me briefly
bird-held to your frame as though
all might be broken; but our bones hold
travelling together in their locking
as I think on it, and that curious
activity they call remembering
biting into us a deeper groove.
Stones have furrows also; it is said
a city can grow from it, a forest.

FISTFUL OF STONES

Caught in the seam of a dress
you'd peeled back to find me,
slouching the high hills as
long as night lasts, tail-ends
of you smear mud on the sill.
Print in a leopard's pad-pad
his search for what is forgotten,
that hinge we made for each other's
cage-door; sounds filter through.
I must put you together again from
impossible fragments; wrist-bone
or blade. Trailing a bird on the
undercliff, pulse in his broken neck
feathers the colour of slow murderous
oceans, blue-grey and sightless;
thought I might lay you to rest
among stones, traveller gone mute
the hardening ribs and heart of you
perfect unbroken fossil-form of flight
clamped between rocks, the shove of tides
or in my heart's chamber, petrified.

LORELEI

Your voice comes like the crackling
spears of lightning I once saw
fracture a mountain.

I was monumental they said
and sang for my supper
like all the blue birds that made it
over the hill.

And then it fell slow like smoke
and I couldn't find you
though my ear leaned and ached.

It was too far down the register
low-tone, earth-knotted.

And I suspended still
in a green oilskin pram
shiftless and waxen, only a silhouette
left to tease you.

So you see your voice is
thicker than breath, is a solid stem of sound
more like bamboo fast-growing
a rod of noise I can cleave to
when silence presses its ugly maw against
my cheek and wraps its monkey-arms to fold me.

When the sweet air is toxic yet
riddles even the call we together make.

OURS

A painter would make this live.
He would know how to look and refuse
the immediate green. He'd rummage
with his eye among the moss, find
yellow, apple-sharp and indigo
until this one cleft sings with
shade you'd never dreamed of.

I am consigned to the edge
a hair's-breadth from paradise
yet so far out the burning bush
is orange as a child's first naming
the donkey is a grey dun animal
and wood is the kind you erect
habitually, forgetting the grain.

I remember you on this coast
though we were never here, your coat
the colour of bee-stings; it still
hangs in the hall. If I am careful
keep watch through all this night
that is like no other, that comes and goes
in our daylight hours, I may find
the particular honey-shade in a single stem
a shaft of dry stick ready
to give the taste of you, though
anyone else would call it straw
and we the dog-day keepers waiting
for the world to come alight

having dipped so far into peat, black moss
and no relief from us. For there can be
no greater pitch than how we fell
when the sun blanked out, how we moaned
and hummed, wrapped in a shadow
no man had seen, something akin to
the way I hated you, angular, deadly
black widow killing each individual blade
precisely: do not remember me thus. . . .

MAROTTE

Let me be low, do not ask the perfect
sentence of me, let not the march of logic
sour my curves nor explanations
catapult my tongue into monotonous
tickings of a metronome; let me not measure
you by this short length nor try to
match my name with yours. I have written
your capital letter, it sends its three
legs tottering across the highway straight
and worthy; I say as they do in the northern
towns, how's that Jack, do you mock me?

Let me lie low and glisten in a snail's
prime. Let me turn about you, watch
where the angle doesn't fit, talk to you
of many ways a man may lay a handkerchief
upon a broken pigeon's neck; how many
shades of grief or love drive my hammer on
sending the nails in deep, hanging life upon
a tree for the wind to fetch it off.
Let my bones rattle in their crazy talk,
do not make a man of me, not carve my features
ready nor names I will have nor itchy feet.
Let me cover the bed with ash and petal
as I think fit and make a sound that befits
a woman come a long way, watching her limbs
fall, each one taken, until the mother gobbles
her heart and nothing is left but a wide-open
vowel and all the shapes and attitudes that

fence it in, and still it must hump and break
the wall down, go roaming for stones where I sit
marking time, rolling my fortune into a cigarette;
let me be smoke, egg, furnace, patchwork and feast.

The land howls at its highest.
I eat stones with a terrible hunger
knowing there is no room for us both
under one skin, feeling the blessed tomb-cold
chill seeping through carnivals and circus-heat
the stink of lion, raucous blood-laugh of a king.

Let me be low, fool, echo, jester,
do not ask of me originals.
Let me laugh when the king does
in a perfect parody; let me sing forth
the many words by which I know
I am not, let me not mate with any
buttoned thing; let me tie ribbons where
they should not, web the beasts together,
prove that impossibles should lie apart,
cusp my own particular under a dock-leaf,
and know the stink of natural kingdoms;
let me not bear another bended child
born to the knee, nor sire a single letter
that will not let the world in; let me be missing
so low down I am a place of stoppage,
a very noxious thing that earns its keep
from below. Let me give rise unto nor
yet impose, not shape the world but stone
my own shape true to keep it upright.

Let me be fervent, devious and angular
bedded and bound, loosened and wrought.
May the embellishments you choose for me
lie easy on, only a finger needed to erase them.
May I come and go among you with a sting
and not the useless hanging purse of deep
instruction; let me not betray you with
pinched lips but send a full-pout kiss
down your eager throat; no half-measures friend,
may I pour, not dribble. You have slid another
perfect egg-shape into my cup, I have spilt yolk
upon our cloth and down my patchwork surplice.
I thank you for my egg love, keep them coming.

TIME THERE WAS . . .

Before the last moan of a trumpet assaults the city
we are still enfolded. Before that particular
stack joins the sky's penumbra. And since
your hand has loosened then, my own arm chills,
creeps into its sleeve; such departures mark
the turning, and where earth waits
for worms and poppy-seed and us when
we let go, before the knife is dry
on her palette, paint still carrying a skin
not solid yet. We could print our initials
right in the middle of all that ochre
she intends for him; I itch to mark you there
in the muddied field she plies and crosses,
long to twist you to a skein and bond
my hair, turn your feet the other way
towards me as the night drones in
and threatens depths we can't negotiate.
Time there was when all these miniscules
of tone and temperature did not erode us
were not snags in the silk, did not part
the heart's membrane in the wrong place
just where it had been stitched against
a deeper wound; could you not leave with such
a spring in your step? Allow a second's
grace between my invitation and its soft decline?
There is little I can call my own today
except an open throat, the smell of melons
a wriggling line of ink trying for shape
on an obstinate page, porous and vital
making molehills where a mountain was.

LOVESICK

When the gods have done with all rank
and exotic varieties of love,
have hacked their way through byways
of a human; have taken hands, heels
humpbacks, craniums for their pleasure
and used up all the sap
to leave dry ditches, pathways of possession
have played their heavenly music
on a shrinking breast, plucked heartstrings for
their every tune and only the instrument persists.

When the gods have had their way
all nuances of love laid bare
for jackals, bones ravished clean
birds still dreaming songs they will sing
when the hunt is done.

When you've dealt the whole pack
pinned the story to the wrong backside
and called love where it is not.
Then can a shuffling begin in the rafters
stems slide into vases, sheets spread
under a hand that knows the lie of land.

Walking the sands in broad day
there may be a stone or a slick of weed
that drowns not in the undertow.
Blinded by war fought in defence of love
buried in excess of maintenance
you raise a thimbleful.
So does a rock, a note, a crimson anemone
flirting in its bowl
dare the extinct and threadbare cloth you are.

MI TANGERE

I find Mariamne just as she disappears.
Any woman, you'd think, might tilt her brim
thus, against so much gold. Mariamne takes
the day for granted but night is a different thing.
Is a hide for stitching, an arrow of sound, bird's
night-shriek piercing the skin, drawing blood or gall.
Only a woman licking the husks of seeds
at the path's extreme length. Not long enough,
my arm waves rudderless in the exquisite lace
of sun translated into shade; it sleeves my skin.
Sister, I call, do not leave me daylight, it is
too bright among us. The merry grins of feasting
visitors hang like daisy-chains between trunks.
I am drunk with you sister, I have a thirst upon me.

REQUIEM

The hills are alive
lux perpetua luceat eis (let perpetual light shine upon them)
the hills are alive with
animas defunctorum (the souls of the departed)
the hills are alive with the sound
de profundo lacu (from the depths of the pit)
alive with the sound of my mother unborn
de ore leonis (from the mouth of the lion)
with the sound of my unborn mother's cries
dies illa, dies magna et amara valde (that day, the great day and
    most bitter)
in the mouth of the lamb in the living hills
in die illa tremenda (on that awful day)
alive with the sound of dying
dies illa, dies irae (that day, that day of wrath)
in the crease of the hills alive with
poenis inferni et de profundo lacu (the pains of hell & the
    bottomless pit)
grass moving, the stain of the herd
dies magna (a great day)
the flock and the crows
Requiem aeternam dona eis, Domine (Lord grant them eternal rest)
the man, the man, my felled mother
quia pius es (for you are compassionate)
he will not come as a saviour to kiss you alive
quando coeli movendi sunt et terra (when the heavens and the
    earth shall be moved)
the man, mother, will put a barrel to your mouth
aeternam habeas requiem (mayst thou have eternal rest)
to hide the sound of silence
de morte transire ad vitam (to cross from death into life)
to hide the silence of agni, agnus Dei
Requiem aeternam dona eis, Domine (Grant them eternal rest, o Lord)

TWO OF US

We will go together up the steep stairs
into the oldest part of the house
where a drip-drip sounds on the sill
and planes haven't been invented yet
so there is no interruption of wood and sky.
I am alive, and we will go
not wishing there was someone with us,
the child, the girl who hung on me
like a sweet tear of honey
or the man who shared my tracks for a while
digging his heels in where I had trod
and the icicles hung on his beard
when we travelled too far north;
it was a long way between us to unravel.
Not wishing for him, breathing like cattle
in the dark curve of fields, not wishing
to lodge in that shell of his shoulder
nor breathe warm all down the length
of this; I am carrying us badly.
The legs fly out, knock things down.
A cup splinters on the edge of time
and I cry out for the broken,
word cracked and creased with so much use
heart failing as we mount the last stair
and glide to a thin white bed
that knows nothing of blood or the rough
                              break-in of birth . . .

THE TRAIN

I

Lavender, it is the colour of hair,
it is spiked with loss and grandmother.
She couldn't catch me a long time
I asked only you. She would run
where light did, tumbling ochre grain
through lassitude, stroking wood, trying to
dislodge your face-print from the handkerchief
I wear like a veil. Her hair
enters my pores with oil spun from a bush.
I have planted it everywhere
in my skin, in the soil, as though
to clear the smutty air of poisons.
Took a while to sweeten my own breath,
chop off the little black barbs
that fringed every word
like you'd break thorns from a stem.
                    (had you tight as flies
                    eye to eye, underfoot)

II

Travelling Virgin, first-class
though I didn't ask for it.
Smoke filters through the grilles
fine as gauze, thin as memory we
didn't ask for, not from cigarettes.
Endlessly the train attendant
pours tea and coffee, *gratis*.
Roast beef, cheeses, crisps and fruits
Chardonnay in miniature, Lakeland water
roll up and down the aisle *sans merci*.
I'm tossed a tiny silver box

in which two truffle chocolates bake
together, one above the other.
Heads droop on virgin cloth,
stuffed owls in daylight.
The table is awash with evidence.
I stare at the trees in flight,
flies dismembered on the glass.
                    (one of them is you)

III

Travelling across the emptiness
going nowhere, there is no water.
I stroke the raised sinews of an arm
in need of flesh. Her tongue hangs,
it is my mother ever thirsty,
killing flies. The barbecue is ready,
we are shackled to each other
each shade a shrunken version of itself
trying to remember who we are.

                    *   *   *

I do not grieve as I eat
cake and truffles, only a rumour.
No one of mine took the train
out east, I've done with feasting
having more than enough of it.

                    *   *   *

Spit if you've any left when trucks
roll in, doors crank open, foetid air,
things crawling too long in each other's
arms for pulse-points, water, recognition.

                    *   *   *

Lingering at the station
I am given my free news,
a hot towel for the sticky film
across my hands, we wipe each other clean.

        * * *

Someone in command marches the platform
orders the hoses wash you down.
Maybe one drop assaults your tongue
outsized limb of pain once used for song.
Now it beseeches, one drop only
less than nothing my mouth to yours.
I stare at the trees; no longer
fugitive they grace the silver snake-tracks
as I lean away from movies, smoke-screens.

IV

Virgin traveller eating my fill
I'm chasing pigs in a fever
rolling in mud the better to know me by,
masking my feral face with lavender
kept with cosmetics in a faux-hide purse
grandmother's blessing pronouncing
life without mercy on the northern line.

KISSING STONES

Hooking an eye is no joke when the basque is tight.
The blind man whirrs and spins like a dying wasp
out of sight. I ply my peachy lace.
Sliding those little teeth into their silver rings
is the effort of an afternoon; he can't see the wood
for trees and wraps himself around coarse bark.
I am not coyly shaping myself beside, he's blindfolded.
When each hook bites, I'm a reformed woman.
He will not dare to eat the peach, gasps fish-like
out of water, expires withal, rather than catch in me.

EPIPHANIES IN HANOVER STREET

The mistress of number six
now she's a sweet one;
drapes the doorway with an outsize
floral blouse, only a coathanger
inside, nothing to speak of.
Never further than the front gate
and even that's a pilgrimage.
She hangs on broken iron trellis
an old sheet thrown there to dry,
sneaks a wafer-thin sliver clinging
to a wishbone from deep down below
where bones are thin as skirt-cloth.
We tell her, pocket-size your meal
taken at dusk with all the street
looking on, breaking bread and her heart
with it, sharing crumbs among birds
and cats, her gathering congregation
uttering one word only angels can hear.

* * *

Pyjamas still in their shiny bag.
The assistant had packed them lovingly
nestled in tissue, soft against soft.
Number ten must walk across town
with the soft votive, bringing to bear
collisions, crossed-wires, artifice
as always and a hole in the heart
that opens and closes like a valve.
She knows, number ten, taking the carrier
from its perch that she'll be pecked at
by the creature who lives in the bed
even as one brushed-cotton sleeve

creeps fearfully along the dead arm
that never lifted a finger.
Buttons shift through their holes
and trousers fight among themselves
to keep the mouth tight shut; he used
to say, thinks she's got diamonds on it.
There is no respite; number ten walks
the centuries to this crustacean
embraces scales as though they were silk
donates herself as sacrifice to the only one
dressing her mother as you might
a bald wooden doll in permanent night.

* * *

Never went to Africa number two
but wears the hat; watches ants
make script on his path, message
drums send under the skin.
Perched on a camel he'd be lethal
riding sunsets like one of those Bedouin.
Now moth-eaten wallflowers hemmed
by snails and the lusty spread
of buttercups tangling his mind.
For didn't he once hold the sun
in his hand and enough fire-power
to light her up? She wore hide
and beads and hair like coal, he
collects signs of her, trophies, tusks
pretending his fade-out concrete plot
is grassland, forest, sand; counts
the hours that sneak among bones
lies to the music blaring from
the window opposite, you're beautiful.

* * *

Couldn't you come Thursday,
couldn't you? I'm nowhere near
the sea, my eyes hurt in winter
light's a funny thing. You wear
what in bed, and something grey?
That's a disappearing colour.
Never walk that far, bed or ocean,
legs get fat and thick, the
ankles swell, no, here a long time
what they call indigenous population
funny there's only one of me.
I do grow something only I forget
its name, it runs green fire
among hollyhocks. Ivy I think
clinging on 'til bricks give way.
Always did wonder why my bones
wouldn't take the weight
thought I don't eat much and they say
no more than a bird she is
when they lift me up. Come soon
then, feel a giddy coming on.

* * *

She lost herself in a tree
the unknown woman who lives at thirty-three.
Greeting her is like talking to a leaf,
she's climbed into the tree's migrant spaces,
faces the street with sap-filled splendour
speaking only with a hush and a shiver
as air moves over her trunk
sleeks her and ruffles her
north or west or spinning compassfuls
flutters her rags like silver-birch
pushes her fit to crack in her bark.

She splits under hands that axe her apart
each time she tries love, each visitor's
mark on walls, sofas, boards, a splash
where the bowl of her skids out of sight.

* * *

Proving the street is a place of angels
number thirteen lifts her chin
with its sprouting hairs and listens.
Numbers twelve and fourteen
also gaze at the sky, hoping to catch
the hem of a heavenly passing.
All they can see are gulls, gulls
and an eyeful; all that reigns here
is a super-abundance of bird
so they turn back inside and close
their doors with a click and a scrape
scoop up the droppings from shoulder
and arse, leave number thirteen
to her own devices; it is not long.
Someone, a stranger, speaks quietly
into her ear, thinking to rescue,
but she hears amiss. Looking to heaven
for an open door, two words only
by-pass the shrieking and wheeling
bore into wax, spiral into her sphere
so never again will the slamming
of gate and the grinding of bolts
lock her dead. Grandmother spoke
through devices, you'd be surprised.
Words like paper planes from a young
                              man's mouth.

* * *

Here he comes. Her ears flap like
a banging door with the latch torn off.
Here he comes, she hears his footstep
on the stair, creak, creak and then
one missing; the shoes he'll unlace
thud of each heavy sole upon boards
planting a bruise in the wood
much like the one she'll wear as
a trophy to school, plastered over.
Here he comes. The voice sneaks into
her blood so she dreams of a liver
thrown on the plate and cut in the shape
of a woman, legs stretched apart
blood oozing into roses. He likes it
in strips fried up with bacon, delicious.
He smacks his lips, and eats.

THE RESURRECTION, COOKHAM

Gravestones, outcrop of frozen cauldrons
leaning into earth, signposts to closure;
eye, heart, limb, a pointing finger
drawn back from function as though
a living hand had pressed each one
backwards in time, to peat, a final *gravitas*
represented by a scarred stone door
refusing access. We are exiled from them.

But look, there is a stirring in the mould
bones knock together, kindling sticks.
Lightning sears stone from within itself
a current fierce enough to blast
and tilt the slabs. One face and then
another, armfuls of lace; the population
claims its village, climbs up again,
swarms of cabbages and kings
run amok in the new sprung churchyard.
No one has a death's head on his
back nor a moth-eaten soul.

They swing on a stony shoulder
having eaten of earth most bitterly
consorted with skulls; or tumble
like a king's loved players
among the grave-flowers, tangled stems
the hearts and minds of unbelievers
open-mouthed, who do not know
how an image breaks with sense
dismisses time like a mangy dog
his tail between his legs.

And in that privilege we call
the painter's eye, a garden works
its way between us, his and ours
dropping seeds like paint or money
arranging for the resurrection
to follow hard upon, just as it always did
and fill the empty churchyard with a congregation.
See, they will not lie down, so he insists.

NOT OURS

They called, light and water
just as his voice skittered
the lake I am, spinning a pebble
shooting in the rough
sending dragonflies sprinting across it
and their wings gaudy rags falling
as my new-found freedom
spins, condenses, ripples out.

She has been taken from him
and the small part that is left
makes a mouth of himself
calling from the bush, the dog's pant
the clump of my boot on the path.

So the river is wide, says the song
give me a boat that will carry two.
The open channel, give me a bow
pushy and stout to part the reeds.
When I was two we shunted thus
upriver, to find the private hollow
earth such as this, our fleeting.

I am dry and bone-thin
as the silk that conquers all
and pays the price. I wear it
like a promise, like the scent
of skin, I am wrapped in him.

He calls, the wrong generation.
An old man in his boneyard
making the table rattle
with his shins awry and bent
as he bangs his spoon upon it.

I cannot, says the voice of me
webbing my foot, making a splash
with my exodus, diving again
for one more pearl from the wreck.

NOW AND THEN

Belovèd, there is a man at my door
he is drowning in himself
so deep I am a woman of lead
or tin, or the substance of light
you can see through
and meet yourself on
the other side.
Once I was wide like
a great full-bottomed boat
and could take
the full fathom five.

Now, when the great weight of oceans
falls upon me
my arms flap like jellyfish.
I am pinned to the shoreline
a mere marker, while his great waves
heave and break on first one membrane
then another. O my so oddly-named lover
you are gone from yourself and the driver
steps down from the cab
rubbing his hands. A great slick
spilled upon my side
the swordfish lick, and you
have tidied up and put on clean cuffs
and are ready for the northern line.

Belovèd, there is a man at my door
who knows not what it is
to linger. Whose finger presses hard
upon me, dialling home
his own phone rings and rings through
empty passages? You watch, my belovèd
weeping that I should lie so, pressed
like heart's-ease into a stiff page, my colours
fierce and brilliant for the collector's eye.

TALKING CURE

White coat, a face stretched
open
he is neat, neat, rubbing the moment up
with great decorum.

She has reached for the laudanum
let it crash
gasps for the moment as though
it were oasis, travelling
each veil, tearing the thin
for what lies
on the other ransacked side.

He sits behind.
Can you go a little further . . .
The contours rearrange her face
into an open, desperate, dying flower
too much unfolded.

And then . . . ?
he says, quiet as the preying mouse
tracking the course she travels
backwards to her own future.

ALTERED STATES

We have begun to barter she and I
and beneath our laughter and sleeping
together like two companionable scallops
we even exchange our dream-beasts
wake with a cockerel clawing a breast
and for me, a squirrel chewing.

Upstairs my bestiaries lie wide open
creatures curving out of the page
to cloak and hook me; I slam them shut
like my dead eye, the other searching
elsewhere, as for instance, I learn
that you are chafed and roar under sedation
that crippling of one's lava
or the vulture's tongue lopped off.

Do you bellow now, not shape?
It is permitted; a poem may rise
formless and gobbling, though
I am carving my misericord precisely
the better to tell you this.

And hard upon, the beasts of war
have trampled across thresholds uninvited,
the mind's lintel, precious front door
wrecked open, while that hidden wrestle
of the spirit with its shadow
takes all one's hours and concentration.

What is it that can ride upon the back
of these invasions? You with your bugs,
I with the kingship of a one-eyed monarch
stricken to the left. And they, the
liberaçion, can only weave a net
to multiply the beasts stalking a story
one man writes to keep himself at bay.

The President exports democracy and freedom
yet is the prime designer of the cage.
You've heard it all before? Dear friend,
never such as this. The ass is abroad
hoof to claw with the jackal.
The sloth is let out and the innocent lamb,
two by two they barter and they wage.

Do not trust these doctors who would mend
the world and end up slaying the variety
of species. Do not trust your own
physician who will caution peace.
Among your herbs and bee-keeping
always room left for thistles; one may weed
a plot to death. I am exchanging feathers
with a friend, you not knowing that my
latest heroine wore hers all night
to keep her father out, call birdwings to her
preserve her right to fly her own migration
though, god knows, there is a universe
of interference when it's chosen.

You will come home, not held upon the edge.
The households wait, a place is laid
at table. All the while I'm able
this ink will run like love or money
to subsidise return; if there are seventeen
words for anger, as the writer says, then
exile is a broken string, an unheard note
peripheral damage; it is also I, unhinged
wishing to loose a pigeon your way
with the right kind of message tied to
                                    its claw-foot.

BEDROOM TOYS

for Carolyn & Peter

Hunting the town's cellars for frivolities
a host of strings you'd thread
through eyelets, draw them tight across
breast or buttock, neat little laces
to gasp among, a feather for your fancy
red kite from the far-off hidden valley
we'll visit one day, the occasional three
or an eagle's longer tickle, hovering
still and treacherous above the eye's sights.
But see, I've left the boudoir, pulled boots on
to go a-mudding for the real thing to roll in.

Down here, your box of tricks would cost
a king's ransom for me to fill it up –
garter or twine, puffball or smoke,
a high-plains drifter wheeling his whip.
Down here among discarded relics, forgotten
souvenirs, what would delight you? A pair
of outsize silken shorts, a garden tool or two
braces, neckties, billets-doux folded tight
in this rusty tin for your unravelling.
My fingers poke and probe among the scraps
curl like cats round each limb's metaphor.
I'd lend you trifles from my bottom drawer
that thing I told you of, scanty and scarce
shocking-pink hairnet I killed him with
silk seams I dare you slither over knees
gone crooked in their prime, something to
button, zip or twist, hook or knot, loop
or rip, stockings to poke a finger through
so much elastic to stretch you both together

and so much lace you'd flee to Nottingham
for mercy; unmentionable tableaux grace
my fever, once on the trail its hard
to let go of texture, volume, scent, exit
backwards from those miniscule emporia
rooms wide open to the street, selling
eye-candy, body-bites, slip of the tongue
as it trawls among exotic flimsies
that have no natural home, to dangle
from the nipple, nose or lobe, secreted
underarm or in some other fleshy crease.

Raking euphoria, clawing for England
I turn to print in search of paradise
and come upon an ancient wedding-song
you'll not decipher, from Albania
Vashez-o, Filez-o, po t'marton, mori,
nana ty – words from an old land to undress by.

KNIFE

For two weeks we have sat at
this same table.
Last time your silver knife
cleaving the air like a fish
darting this way and that
as your mind charts it, how far you are
from the still centre, marked by a tiny plate.

We were using the table to talk, the salt
an unscaleable tower, the plate smeared chocolate
two plump truffles you slice to smaller pieces
until only a sliver is left, and even that
you must share between us
all the while speaking of leaving the earth untouched
buried cache, a seam unmined.

Though it is rivers we spoke of
the fish was easy on this air
turning across the plate, blade tracing
code as it points
and pulls the chocolate dust asunder –
this crucible holds all our hunger.

See, we are still here, we never left
did not coil together as the implements suggested
did not take food that lay beyond our feast
are still heaving metaphors into place
playing patience with a fish-bone.

I have fought all evening with this carcass
drawing off tiny flakes, a child's portion.
I concentrate, it is a fool's game
satisfying appetite along this narrow ridge
of bone. I remember you allowed
a brief hug last year, your fine-boned shoulder
searing my sense, a living wheal
of knotted fibre on my heart.

Beyond the rim, this fish's skeleton
picked clean, our mountain ridge
is swathed in mist, my words
sheep's wool snagged on some fence between us.
Once more we're truffle-bound,
you slice the white again, again, again
until I am thin. This time
your blade holds two small clinging
sweetnesses on one side and the other.
Together we draw sugar from the steel
our life pared down to final pickings.

It is late, we leave, the moon is promise
and heavy, ominous, swirling clouds.
In the fish-wife's song, cockles and mussels
                              alive, alive-o. . . .

BEFORE

Until I have dusted down the wicked
crenellated breaks in my heart's masonry,
until I have turned your face to the corner
broken the dreadful stare of a divided moon
forced you to gaze on dust, twin element
that you are; until I have pulled that distant star
back into orbit and named it as my own constellation
or driven myself back to the old bald centre,
the blasted terraces where no shoot lives
or earth uplifting, yet unripened knots still shifting
below, amiss in their muzzled nudge for breakage.

Until I have counted the three-fingered man
among my fellow devourers or hung from a bleached sky
like an old lantern faulting and stuttering
in deep and unheard nights; until I have rocked
you awake oh my baby, birthmarked with me,
have swabbed clean your flesh of match and copy.

Until I have banished the great lie of naming
listed my masks along paper sheets too stretched
for a morning, tidied the album's gallery of thieves
and found a way to believe my grandmother's
foot trod me down for my own sweet good
or begetting, to know where the edges are
of her floral soul held in the weave of
an apron; we inch up in spite of dalmations
mother's chiffon and papa's old pipes
that wheeze in the back room for thimblefuls
of air, one at a time until we are ten or twenty
until we are grown and counted like grains of sand
on a foreground that's gone out of fashion.

Until I open the window, drawing it up like
a great lidded eye, then no birds sing.

AMONG THE BIRDS

1 *Striptease*

Take a glove, white, the length of an arm
for the box of bedroom toys is hungry
and we're stuck for a new sensation; so take
a garment hard to unpeel it's so enamoured
of its host and tightly cloven. What kind
of sleek familiar leeches up the skin,
waves or points, strokes or indicates –
have you ever taken it on the chin
from a white satin fist rhinestone-knuckled
so it punches neat little slices out of you
like you cut yourself when shaving?
That's the excuse, you'd prefer to have it off
except there's an art to that like everything.
It is a glove I say, nothing more, not
stocking, garter, basque, stiletto, g-string.
Gloved, the hand teasing round the drawing-room
looking for the exit, wrist turning clockwise
timing you limb by limb, measured invasion,
a whole new dimension to the naming of parts.
Gloved is a word that tells you lights-out
stealth and virtue, hints at a long haul
from entrée to disclosure. Taking a stitch
at a time, you pare off the white silk membrane
so she bleeds, though not a glass is broken.

2 *Discard*

The frozen cast a fallen angel at your foot;
you take it up, a jewelled circus-limb
swinging from your thumb. Within that musty
cave the trace of tarnished sweat-prints like
a rusty nail's assault, marking nightgames

like stations of the cross, erotic calvary.
Let it fall again; it buckles, flattens, lies,
love's negotiation branded in a crease, hinge
of the wrist a mountain-ridge you fell from.
You have her now, a pool of artifice;
using a stick you poke the animal about
flayed and preyed upon, its skin a twisted
replica of action – a beckoning, a promise,
that beaten hide your once exquisite guide
to what the foliage and gesture mystified.

3   *The Word for It*

Soon another glove arrives,
chrysalis once occupied, still
guarding history's mould and tenure.
This, with the fingers bent upon
themselves like rabbits' ears
flat to the head; imagine
how a creature close to ground
hearing the thud of foot and gun
among the wheatstalks, dread
might beat its heart upon enduring.
I can't unbend it, coming stitched
but mangled, something worried
by a dog; so many twists and folds
in leather, it is a thing fallen
between names, our battered glove
worked to the bone by all those
wooden toys and games cut short,
the tumbrels of a nursery-chest.
Coming to a crossroads; the cat
drops a still-shrilling bird
its broken legs upended on
the polished pampered boards,
some vast and creeping negative

captures both twisted forms on floor
and table, binds them beyond all sense.
We have only this: brown, hide, feather
for a living – the world's glove
where this misshapen carcass cannot.

4   *Homing*

Press your hand slowly into a pouch
of skin; it gives, allows and copies
what you do, tracing the long and
curious journey to the fingertips.
It is the occupation of the air
a child demands, breaking in to breathe
its new and close-knit covering.

5   *The Days*

The glove, master of indication
soft insinuating tool of interruption
arrows along the horizontal
of my sight, masking the lilies.

Little net mitt, you are scarcely
glove, if it's love we are speaking of
too many holes in you, too many
snags catching, or letting through.

Black hide, loose fit, fist for earthing
thick as falcon's claw, outsize cuff
stubby and short, peel for the fruit, thou
preventer of union, let me into the rough.

Glove fetishist to parrot-fancier:
don't let them natter you into
a single issue, there's more variety

of species in this kingdom
than a gaudy bird or two.

I know a hawk from a handsaw
gauntlet from claw, though the wind
be howling wild enough to sever.

She said, he could read from the inside
skin of a glove how the owner would sound
in a cave without light, feeling only
the encroaching hand of the gloveless.

He could trace that valley between
thumb and index, curve of delight
where the hand parts company
with itself, gives way to the soft
interior of a skin-clad palm.

6   *Dancer*

The blind choreographer
has no need of them.
Even a Russian winter
cannot paralyse that hand
pressed to the boards marking
each dancer's beat; each *pointe*
a note upon his stave
the fingers lit with sound.
He wears a knitted comforter
over his ears; the hands fly
multiplying plié, arabesque.
In the kingdom of the blind
a gloveless man is king.
In the land of no sight
a master hand the eagle.

The man and woman in designated roles
enact the ritual of their aftermath;
inevitable sacrifice of so intense
a passion, it consumes each one to ash.
And in each charred and decimated soul
the gods still rage and fart and copulate.
Here, on my left, I draw the gauntlet on
to better take the dare of hawk or falcon,
grip of a claw fit to tear the heart
out of a man; the glove's concession.
While on my right, a sweet pretence
articulates the nuances of love
its creases, valleys, cracks; so does
the leather bend to tend a sparrow
this glove an intimate of skin,
wife, sister, child and close enough
to fool the world, the hand that bears it.
Rough cousin, smooth blood-kin, I have
you both now on each untethered limb.

LEAVING THE BIRDS

Where a twig breaks
evening grows upon
each stalk, masters it;
where the rutted path
drives sure as wolves
dividing seagrass
evening-lit, so let us
gather this side
of paradise to know
the tread, print, verb
track the lower
kingdom of us.
We are two, three, four
a prime quartet
seeking wine
an arrow's length
from footstools.

* * *

Necessary sometimes
to bite the bullet
spread like starfish
on the earth, not
posed as gardenware
urn or yarrow, table
burnt with sun, no,
sprawl, dismantle
fall among the poppies
feel grass with the
inside of a thigh
lick catlike through
an afternoon, taking
the bend in time
like an angel loosed
from the pen, scratching.

* * *

You with your dark wise eyes
just there on the blue wooden
chair tucked in to this angle
of flint, clematis promising,
release the gods who plague
our solitude, must needs
rip off the mask; bared teeth
and witchery. You caught
my fragile knowing, gave it
root; last night my friend
searching trench-maps, found
a name, married word to
furrow, and so recovered in
a place of joining where
he meets with his own self.
And my most feared unveiling
hers and mine, is dragged
from mire and given
pride of place; theatres
part their curtains
and the gods take centre
stage for our release.

A quiet Sunday, no more
significant than ash.
We turn the embers, fall
from grace, make gargoyles
of our pleasure-giving face
and fall, head-over-heels
to turn the matter on its head.
Trying for heaven is a fool's
game; where hell is found
better to know your way around.

SMALL TALK

Your hair is the same
colour as the leaves of
that bush, I hope
our paths, our crosses
pass and do not crack...
See here Jack I meant
to lean upon your note
but you are writing what?
Libretti these days and
can't hear the common word.
Long time since I had
a gentleman's umbrella
hanging in my hall...so
why not come and fetch it
if you catch a slice of
me, count myself lucky
sitting beneath librettists
and an eager professorial
whine to be enraptured.
Soon if I wait long enough
will some smile crease
a feature, let sap flow up
and we can mingle dew-ponds
with a tricky summer, loose
ends, tried to tell, gathering
them up, you know, a winter's
tale badly out of season;
but here is summer to infinity
negotiate the rose, the lyric
scene, his hat a shade to conjure
with, the circle closed by common
currency, a barbarous child
let in with curls for keys

the adult slammed for
having no good thing to say
except those loose ends
trailing bush-hair, cellists
vocal pyrotechnics, who shall
come among us lest he walk
on water, cover all the points
deal an ace, make a face
giving none away himself
included, so, I bid farewell
that's clear, correct & mute
entire, acceptable; next day
the right card rattles into life
such a lovely afternoon, yours…

YOURS

Somewhere near, no more than
a few streets away, a beacon or two,
in the valley of, the shaded place
a starburst deep in the bloodwarm
cave of her, advancing, settling;
love, begotten, just as the dust
rises from my tomb, who gave her
free to the world upon her coming.
So she now, soft, with full-blown
coil of flesh unto its own,
cups and covets, gnaws on the wind's
cruel knuckle, finding meat
to feed that grain, a cell
of wonders cleaving to her centre.

I can hear the call, my own blood
quickens; feel the nudge of all our
routes and scales; this is a
universe of knots. I tie you safe
in love, though you are winging out
to know the messages your seed beats
through us all, those of us who
do not claim you as their own
can feel the shape pressing on your bone
a shadow still, a name, or wish
annunciation broad as the donkey's
back to bring us to the crux.
Small crystal, take your own time
it will come, the note you are
your howl of triumph, an angel told me so.

ADVENT

In the light of five candles
on a misshapen, balded tree
needles fall, soft barbed truths
to blot the earth out
sifting downwards to the root.

This advent I lugged my
old friend down from its perch
in the steeped, flint-terraced
garden, awash with expectations.

Always we wait, the year's nadir
denser each time we sink
into its mouth; this time, another
presence seeps into the room.

She comes, no messianic burst
from heavenwards or Gabriel's
forewarning; no word escapes
to hint of it, only her weight
has shifted, the gravity undone
one captured button less
mysterious swell we cannot see
but only circle ritually, speaking
in tongues, a tethered melody.

Gawain on the wall, his face
a rapture of intention, valiantly
coming forth to crack our frozen seas.

My daughter also, crossing
the spirit-line, crouches deep
in my flesh, worn tonight
like crumpled feathers, pride
of place, a canny Baptist
crowing the path open, serving
supper fit for a king.

Now she sings of it within
her hand cupped like the guardian
she is, to cheat the melting wax.

DEARLY

The still small voice cleaves
like thin smoke from a bed
deep in arcadia; there is
an arrow true and straight
to her, not to be spoken
as though the jaws gobbling
up my life have had their
fill at last; as though
my own fast is broken
upon this note, my mother's
song a falling scale of bone.

Sinking so far into herself
she's no one, yet I hear it borne
upon the wind, ancient voices
of the child she was, marking
time to save herself from moaning.

She chews grapes, spits them.
They have landed on my skin
and turn it green, it is
green fire speaking upon me
a burn too fierce to see.

That was the bed, the island;
hands stray like crabs
to find the shoreline; there is
an expedition in this visit
though the nurse won't catch it.

I hold the receiver tight
use a lover's words to
fold her loose and too-wide
wish her back unto its own,
take out my hard-won stone
and sharpen up love's knife;
late now for feeble gestures
send my heart hot down the line
for chewing on, knowing it lands
but no geography, nothing of that
boundless offering left to see.

Too far out she is for any
contemplation; there are laws
it seems, beyond cognition, too
vast and tremulous not to obey her
nor submit this moment's grace to
                              things undone.

THE ORB OF INFLUENCE

We are two, plucking our items from thin air
to feed the mystery; or burrowing deeper
than a probe to send out movement
miniscule, tethered, from the inner sea.
We, you and I, are ship and cargo
lap and innocence; we breed our infancy
again, coming upon ourselves before these
words are formed, powerhouse of inwardness,
buried princess, a tide not yet momentum,
bedded-in and flexing in that hollow,
crucible. Stars roam here, fingers
too small to hold; a dragonfly will shimmer
on the cake, the match is lit, we come
to gather hands unto our own and lend
a hand; someone is hungry for this
and writes it, more than spectator, my
progenitor, a scribe of wizened width
gaining an inch or two each week
speaking the world from a tear on her cheek.
Lost and found, she sends her script
for exorcism, deep in the groove
where we two breathe one night,
this orb sending its light out to those
who still search underground for mercy
while we lodge in the mind's fishbeds,
                              our catch.

TRYING FOR CLOVER

Time passes, things intervene.
Such as snow falling in spring
disguising the fragile, such as
a room you can't ignore smelling
of distance, where she creeps
so slowly into her own cloak
her head still rising to receive
some hard-found word or two
drawn up as from a well like
grace or gift, small capture.

I am tethered to her for this
last epiphany never seen before,
bend my ear close to hear her
speaking strive to shape itself
within me; pleasure you are here
she says, mouthing all she can be.

You, my grown girl, are waiting
in the wings of my theatre
angered that your scene is not
yet come, that I must turn
to this arrangement of my heart.
You fear contamination, as though
you are not buried deep within
this season, beating your life
up through my bones, taking
the corridor at a pace to where
a life slows; inventing futures
in her hollows your child leaps.

The shadows lengthen, it is soon
upon us. I see my features fourfold;
bone-wrought and cavernous,
a mother's almost stone-cast face.
Afloat in mirrors my multiple
deceivers and aslant your smiling
where the event is promised, she
undercover yet and swimming for her
life, oceans to fight through,
no light nor house, no shoreline
gap or gate to guide us easy in.

BEHOLD

Kraków, 2005

It is not that I found
a poster advertising Lorca and
didn't tell, or a plaque for the home
of the communist party, and did.

Nor discovered my tarnished
aristocracy that yet steers
a course across cobblestones.

It is not that I did the acceptable
thing and gained the museum in
a crumbling step or two, then fled
from its hush into the barb and shrug
of that square I can't get away from.

It is not that I lost my
way and the potholes caught
me greedy for filling in.

Nor that a knowing
that comes from beneath
guided the flight.

Nor is it nosing upstairs for
Christmas decorations in high summer
or counting baubles in place of men.

It is not that american voices
took no notice preferring
their mobile phones

and the small polish couple
on the sofa behind engaged
with me from the backbone.

It is not that nothing was said all
day except to a waitress and the green
cloth she laid to serve my
norwegian fish reminds me of envy.

It is not that the streets stopped
inviting and I needed another
pair of shoes to open them up

though not with laces missing
and different sizes
according to where they fell.

Nor that I cried only once
in the place
where rivers would not be enough.

It is not that the great glass tanks
of tangled hair held also
perfect plaits, a whole head taken

nor the tiny clothes of infants
deceiving us with silence.

It is not that the daily ration
was laid awesome out, feastless
under a glass cover

nor that I shone my torch to
track one floating spear of matter
whose name is forgotten.

Nor the reduction, the
scales, the bone poking through.

It is not that the tongue
is out, the gruel too thin

nor that words perish
in the backwoods, the bud,
his lower spine.

If this be a man his tongue
cannot lap or utter.

It is not that he is yet dog
but falls in between.

Nor that I haven't
any good thing to say

nor clue, nor good
companion on the way

though we walk in the form of
obeisance to this darker than,
and the most warped corners
of our souls are beaten.

It is not that we are beyond
utterance or intelligence or stutter

nor that the birds still shrill
here among poplars and birch.

It is a kingdom of negatives
this, not to be taken.

Nor that the print is not close
enough woven, just that to fall
through the stolen is no requiem

where notes cleave too tight
as flesh that is bright and molten
nor that your arm in mine isn't hooked as kin.

TO SEAMUS, YOUR FIRST DAY

Sunflower a fine backbone to this beginning
the sky a burst of firelight branching down.
She weeping water to tell of threshold,
it is come, we are ready, I must part from you.
And silence is bestowed upon the time
rings as though air itself were stricken.

Small, like you in the slumbering flesh
that was cut for you, I am attending
to the mesh and tackle of my heart
like Russian sailors, fathoms deep
and running out of air; tides tug,
shift forward, down, I grope as you do
blind on the sea's bed to mouth and find.
Little one, I'm word-locked, knowing no
name, reaching stars for the sense of you.

She has become a great geography
a land you curl into; her hair falls
across the small globe of your head
brushing nightmares off before they bite.
You are becoming less than night,
you howl and whimper, composing operas
crescendos, lamentation; I listen closer,
you are a note beyond the ear, a single
bell pealing, I only catch vibrations,
tremors of glass or curtain, the wise
wind sending sound I cannot hear, music
not printed yet to tell me who you are.

Surely you are lost in her, yet serve
your own sweet purpose; landslide,
mountainous, she rides each hunger
with the grace of queens. How shall I
carve this undiscovered contour, eden
she is now, towering over you an ark
a house, a mansion; and in her bending
to your gaze, that stem we started with
is bone to hold your head, her hand
the hinge to keep you all together.

HOLD

for Seamus

I bring a sound from the high slopes
bell against loss, those mountain-keepers
held by a rope of far-off notes
tethered to shepherds, hill-farms
or one lone caller here, drawing you in.

And your eyes grow wide, staring
into me and out beyond us both
to a wide, wide world uncharted yet
cupped by this hollow beat on metal
mountain-goat's familiar, echo, deep-song.

SNOWDROPS FOR SEAMUS & ME

The grey is easy, quiet, as though a pause
among stones, press upon the spirit.
This time of year when I remember the
dreaded length that dead can be, with
no crying. Have I ever told you this,
how that well of grief is equal music
to our laughter? It is the no-note time
that kills, and deadens every reach
where no birds sing. I follow my king
to his hovel; here under ash and the
trial of conversation, a wooden hut
is laid with hanging heads of white
as though the flower were shamed in
green and moss supports it. And she had
lit the candles there, leaping among
those purest flowers. I am reminded
on a dark day, my house dispersing, a world
of pieces, on the move, someone may gather
moss and cluster, invite attendance on
a company of flowers whose life is kin.
Within this hour I cross a mountain,
carry a small white treble to
my grandson, threat the monumental with
a fragile, write to Lucy that it is
a thing to do, this day, and light it.

LOVE OF COUNTRY FLOWERS

for Lucy

On Saturday I fought with
crowds of lilies she carried
to my door; you were not there.

On Sunday grappled with a
size and perfume greater
than comfort; they topped even

the largest of my jugs
and woodlice scuttled fear
full back into their element

while I grasped for air; lilies
abounding in this tiny house
their breath reminding me

that too great gift is
less than nothing; to drown
in scent is no experience

and all the overblown must
die sooner; she meant well,
her conversation was as

fully-throated; you with silk,
hardy perennials, did not show
your face and Monday comes,

the days march on until a week
is passed; and once again I
am among the ordering of plants

their fine arrangement, named
and talented; we speak of Anna
and her scarlet women, loose

upon the Flintstone, in precision.
We processed beneath the arch
their pattern is the march

of blossom on the wind, a grey
and scarlet company trying
their bones upon resistant air.

Today snowdrops are gone; within
your shed air thickens, coalesces
on a jug and such a crown of

fragile stems as I would weep for.
They are mine; again I carry riches
in a ragged, rough bouquet, and

weightless. Why, when I know so
little of you, do I sense the mettle?
A whole field sings among us.

THE YEARS

Going to ground as the stealth
of fox, as it could be fox
yet more like small seeds
rolling in grass, turning
the next move over, remember.

Coming to ground, sight of
a river as though looking down
on the child we once were,
boats moored and ready; I pulled
with you once on this inland water.

You who begat me and you who
took me under, boats heaving hard
upriver; my husband, my father
you knew not how hard it was
to know both of us dark-drowned.

Coming to ground, Ted, your best
poem ever, reading mine as you sank
into nothing but bone; my words,
you said, deep shafts of light.
Strange how luminous one is to another.

Coming here, where my grandmother
stood at the apex of us, her sisters
like birds, their wings ever ready,
spines of thin bone their ribbons
stitches and hooks, their arms I learned

to leap from. It is the mount of summer,
there is no more to raise or keep risen.
Daughter, though I dance with your son
down my years, there is none who would
interfere now, as I cross firm over

and know that words must never answer
nor swing from the margins or act out
the story; but come in hesitant and temporary,
oblique and canny, lighting only the frame,
grace as a lining like moss for their turning.

The wind takes longer now to bite.
From my window, to one side, water.
My back to the swell, I drift in
our shallows, as though there may be
scent or scarab or stranger here.

Just as now words sound like bells
within a cathedral, before air disperses
and ears that catch and mould them.
Once I hammered vowels into forms like
a smithy; now from a vault, they speak me.

SEVENFOLD

And they all bent over their honeypots
and a great silence fell upon the face of the table.
And the Lord said, lo! I have given honeypots,
let there be satisfaction among the tribes.
And he waited and waited even unto eternity, saying:
why are there no gruntings and snufflings
among my people, and turned his face away from the earth
so troubled was he by the silent dipping and spooning
leaving his people to their own devices.

While Barnaby scoured his honeypot with a cello-bow
naming his eating The Pig Concerto.
Victoria dug and dug deep in her pot, saying burn, burn
while John ran amok among the roses.
And James sat mute having lusted after more than one
but fearing to seem unseemly in his greed, took his slowly.
Dora surveyed the table, noting the angle of each elbow and spine
drawing her own conclusions like unto the Lord.
Mine hostess ate with a twinkle having stolen it from the cellist
in inappropriate places, even unto the tennis-court.
While John piled ashes of burned roses in his empty pot
for Vicky's delight, his honey turning grey among the company.
More! she cried in his two stung ears
for they had made sure the bee-story followed on
it being a time of hives, swarms and the trading of honey
though the Lord being turned away did not upturn the table.
And Sarah leaned, taking it on the chin, her chocolate hit
bending to let it in and casting the pleasure forth across the cloth
in full collaboration, the enemy being routed
though there was no horde or sword among the people.

The Lord sighed, his gift translated sevenfold
and seven pairs of eyes (less one) seeing the emptying of their own
returned to digging in each other's honey
for one small pot is not enough for such as these.

POCKET

What is this dust in my pocket's seam?
Last remains of a man I once knew
fondled in flesh, twisted to a universe of curves
turned inside-out. Have I held you back
with these shards of opulence, flakes of hunger,
traces of occupation, furnace, capture;
ash between the rollers of my fingers probing
the hidden weave; above, a surface currency
travels through this cavity, visits, vanishes
is lodged and spent, my pocket bearing
treacheries, alliance, theft and innocence,
a stolen letter, perfume of ancient petals,
a child's curl, a pen that wrote you out.

Beneath this transience, deep in the crease,
a more substantial presence clinging on
dark corner so far down the name dissolves
burnt-out and cooling, filtered through cloth,
my pocket's memory, no more than a fingerful
as though to not allow this last of you
to fall out of mind; as if these dusty traces
were your whole person, upright, running from fire
for your life, as my fingers turn and sift
all I knew, packed tight in the heart of me.

LETTER TO M

I thank you, sir, for your indulgences.
My heart was ever wanton at your side
But now is tamed of all its old excess
And in its own house will, forthwith, abide.

Holding the phone's receiver for too long
And for my sake, since I can't get to you
Provides a threat of laughter, as a song
Might break the course we are committed to.

O that my dark may soon divide to let
The earth and all its wonders deep inside.
I have a taste of it, and love you yet
Though time will part us, as my life grows wide.

Would that the nameless seeds and night-time moths
Are good companions, as you've been to me
In all these meetings, crossings, thresholds, wraths –
I am, sir, quite o'erwhelmed by what I see.

So pen these phrases, with some little shame
Yet wish to honour our just cause outright
To put the matter in its proper frame
And shed some joy where once was only blight.

To end upon a note, 'tis badly done
That I profess the love I feel for you
And who you are and all we've ever known
Except in these few words, a lesser view.

NIGHT WORK

A particular morning, nothing to speak of
wind underground, a distant rumble
under the shoe, occasional drift as
grass bears its passing; my rosemary
stands like cathedrals, cascades of frost
still flowering and purple this October.
Yet more is folded there, the loop and hook
of webs, as though hung from above
dropped and caught on the spiky pines.
This soft night-knitting festoons my eye,
I travel all over this bush I never
knew, as though a hand had drawn and etched
it just for me; each thread sears the green,
fine rib-bone, a fragile net, a perfect symmetry.
A dozen spiders worked all night for this
and hang, each one, the heart of stillness.

MAGPIE

I always did love the blues
that deepening rasp of throat or string.
We are steeped in blue notes from
the dusk of our minds' penumbra
to the place where a fox might lie
in daylight, shadow-pocked in the land.
She has stitched and shaped him
draws out his stealth in the scratch
and scrape of our pens as they worry the page,
the cloth, tease at particulars; we have known
in this afternoon's abundance, outside & inward
the way a quilt can carry you across
a continent, the breathing of a creature beyond sense.
We have found tense and tension, an architect's fine-tune,
the tucks and knots, tracks and trace of thread
and skein, the age of indigo, the way
that colour shifts and salts the spectrum
nudging up to red and ochre, sending shadows
through the palette, humming, tinting, smouldering,
the seepage of a blue too complex for one day's
inhabiting; we wear our Joseph-coats to better
trawl the length of it, kick it aside, find its disguises.